Published by Sausage Dog Publishing
PO Box 259, Stamford, PE9 9AT

Sausage Dog
Publishing

© 2006 Sausage Dog Publishing
www.happyhandz.biz

Designed by dsquared Ltd.
www.dsq.co.uk

Printed by
Hicking and Squires
Unit One
Engine Lane
Moorgreen Ind. Park
Moorgreen
Nottingham NG16 3QU

ISBN 978-0-9554932-0-1

Contents

Foreword by Siân Lloyd

The British are often accused of being lazy when it comes to learning languages.

If you tell people you are studying another lingo, the ones that spring to mind are usually French, German or Spanish. However, in the UK, many people are unaware that right here on our own doorstep we have access to four home-grown languages.

After English, Scots-Gaelic and Welsh there is another language that is unique to these shores: British Sign Language or BSL for short.

As someone who is a fluent speaker of both Welsh and English, I believe it is important to promote and encourage the use of our native languages, both spoken and non-verbal.

In my role as a broadcaster, I am very aware of the vital role that communication plays in all our lives. Whether it's waiting at the bus stop discussing last night's television with a stranger, or a mother making eye contact with her baby, communication is the basis of all human relationships.

In order to understand each other it is important that we can communicate successfully.

Surprisingly, though, communication is not only about words. The actual words we use account for only seven percent of the message. The other 93 percent is made up of non-verbal communication such as the tone of voice used, our facial expressions and our body language - they all help to give our words their true meaning. These are gestures that everybody uses almost instinctively. Have you ever tried to direct a lost motorist to a particular destination without using your hands to get your point across?

Imagine if you could somehow build on these natural gestures and shape them into a cohesive, structured communication system that would enable you to have effective two-way communication with your child.

Welcome to the wonderful world of sign language.

All children love using sign language because it is a natural, stimulating way to communicate that can be learnt so easily.

This book is an easy-to-understand introduction to sign language that is readily accessible to parents and carers with young children. Through the use of simple stories and clear graphics, Garry has provided those interested in learning more about this beautiful and expressive language with a clear and straightforward introduction.

BSL is a language of which all British people, whether deaf or hearing, should be truly proud.

> Children love using sign language because it is a natural, stimulating way to communicate that can be learnt so easily

Siân L

SIÂN LLOYD
TELEVISION PRESENTER

Olli says:
Did you know that 93 percent of communication is non-verbal?

Introduction by **Garry Slack**

Olli says: Join me in helping your child learn over one hundred signs through our four action-packed stories.

Imagine the benefits of being able to communicate with your child at such an early age. Your children will be able to give vent to their feelings and communicate their needs through the beautiful, expressive and visual medium of British Sign Language.

Most sign language courses and instruction books concentrate on learning individual, often unconnected, signs. From my own experience of learning sign language, I am only too aware of how difficult it is to learn a new language while trying to remember a list of seemingly unrelated signs. It was because of this that I decided to choose signs that would be relevant for young children and their carers and weave them into a series of stories that would help the reader to both learn and remember the signs.

With this one unique book you can learn signs that are relevant to the everyday needs of your children, while following and enjoying the adventures of Olli, The Little Monkey, and his family.

During the course of four action-packed stories in this book, you will learn over one hundred signs, from British Sign Language, that will help you to communicate better with your child. This enhanced dialogue helps both you and your child to reduce the stress and complications of everyday life, and to build strong bonds for the future that effectively improve understanding.

The book is illustrated throughout with photographs showing how to produce the signs used in the stories, plus charming illustrations of Olli and his family and friends which all help to bring the stories to life.

Thank you for buying this book. I hope you will enjoy learning the signs and benefit from improved communication with your child.

Why use sign language?

Research has shown that all babies use some signs whether they are nodding or shaking their heads, waving hello or pointing at a favourite toy. These are natural signs understood by everyone.

What is not so widely known in the UK is that because the muscles in a child's hands develop before those needed for speech, all babies, both hearing and deaf, can be taught and encouraged to communicate pre-verbally with their parents and carers, by using sign language.

British Sign Language, or BSL as it is more commonly known, is the first language for approximately 70,000 people in the United Kingdom.

Unlike the spoken languages traditionally taught to children, such as French and German, sign language is a natural and easy-to-learn second language. BSL is now recognised as the fourth indigenous language of the UK and it is being increasingly used in pre-school settings and in the rest of the educational world.

All of the signs used in this book are borrowed from BSL, although I have adapted some of them to make them easier for children to produce and recognise.

Learning signing as a second language improves children's communication skills and, unlike other signing systems which are often limited in their vocabulary, BSL is a complete language that you and your children can continue to learn and use together - making it easy to communicate in places like noisy playgrounds, supermarkets and parks.

Children love learning sign language as it is a very stimulating, fun and visual medium. And many youngsters can pick it up pretty quickly.

Olli says: Sign language is a fun and stimulating medium. Children love to learn sign language.

Benefits of signing

- The benefits of signing with babies and toddlers. Using sign language to communicate with pre-lingual babies and young children has become very popular in the USA. Research has shown that signs allow babies to share their feelings and thoughts with their carers long before they are able to use speech.

- The benefits of baby signing. Babies learn to communicate pre-verbally. All babies communicate instinctively using natural gestures such as nodding and shaking their heads for yes and no. Parents and babies all use a limited form of sign language to communicate. Learning formal sign language helps to build on this foundation.

- It is the bridge between non-verbal and spoken language. Vocal chords do not develop fully for intelligible speech until the age of 12 to 18 months, but the tiny muscles in a child's hands develop before those needed for speech. This means a child can learn to communicate using sign language before being able to speak.

- It encourages early language development and understanding. Between six and nine months old, babies begin to understand that objects have names. Signs help babies to make sense of the words that they hear every day.

- It takes away the guesswork. Imagine if your child was able to tell you about the big red bus going past the window or that they had hurt their knees falling off the slide. Sign language helps children to communicate their observations and feelings about the world around them with their parents or carers.

- It strengthens the bonds between children and carers. Because you are able to communicate with your children at an earlier age you are able to understand their feelings and thoughts. This leads to a stronger relationship with your child, and your baby will soon learn that he or she is able to communicate with you more effectively by signing rather than resorting to crying. This increased communication will reduce the tears and tantrums that so frequently arise due to the inability to communicate with one another.

- It increases babies' language development. Many people worry that by using signs a child's language development will be slowed down. In fact the reverse is true. Research shows that learning to sign does not limit the development of speech - indeed it enhances a child's communication skills. Children who can sign often speak earlier than children who do not use signs.

Above all... IT'S GREAT FUN!

Hints & Tips

This book encourages total communication - the use of voice and sign to maximise communication. The signs are used to support the spoken word, so remember when you use a sign say the word at the same time.

Repetition is the key.
The more babies see the signs the more they will become familiar with them, and be able to produce them.

Facial expression and body language are important. Try to look happy and use your body, as well as your hands, while you sign. Remember to vary the tone of your voice depending on the context. It is no good saying "good boy" unless this is matched by the tone of your voice, your body language and the expression on your face.

- Try to make signing a part of everyday life.

- Use just a few signs to start with. Good ones to begin with include Milk, Food, Again and More.

- Meal-times and changing times are good opportunities to introduce signing.

- Get eye contact with your child before signing.

- Don't be disappointed if your child does not make a sign correctly. Keep signing and saying the word in the right way to give your child a chance to copy you.

- Try to be patient. It may take a few weeks before your child makes his or her first sign.

- Use lots of praise.

- Learning a new language can seem daunting at times but remember that all the time you are improving your child's communication skills - so keep persevering.

- Make learning signs the best of fun with your child, by using the stories, songs and rhymes.

- Get everyone involved. Sign language is great fun, so get all the family to learn the signs.

Olli says: Don't forget to be patient and keep praising your child. Sign language is real fun.

Daisy - a true story

Hilary is the proud mother of Daisy and works at a school in Cambridgeshire, where she is the head of modern languages. This is her experience of using sign language to communicate with her daughter.

Daisy signing the word for duck.

Daisy pointing at the ice-cream van.

The learning begins

I learnt a few signs from a friend who signed to her little boy. The signs I started with were: Milk, Change Nappy and Duck (feeding the ducks on the local pond was part of our weekly routine.)

I signed these all the time, mostly with the purpose of getting me signing. When Daisy started weaning, I added: Food, Drink, and More. One day, when Daisy was seven months old, and did not want her breakfast, I signed Milk. She stopped crying and the widest smile lit her face. Wow!

I extended my range of signs by attending Garry's baby signing classes. Daisy started signing back to me when she was ten months old. She just went for it, all in the space of one day. Her first sign was Milk and her second was Duck. Several others followed that day. When it was time to go, I signed Home and she crawled over to her car seat and climbed in.

Bathtime fun

But our real breakthrough came at bath-time. Daisy's father came out of the bathroom asking: "What does this mean?" Daisy had been trying to tell her father she wanted some milk. So if a ten-month-old could remember a few simple signs then daddy should be able to as well, especially if he wanted to be in on his daughter's first attempts at structured communication with the family.

Through baby signing I can see that Daisy makes connections between words and ideas. For example she signs food at the mention of breakfast, tea, lunch, or eating.

One morning I actually regretted teaching her to sign because when I told her we were off to nursery she signed Home back to me. The nursery staff also told me that one day, when they were bringing the children in from the garden, singing Old MacDonald had a Farm, Daisy put a fist up to her nose - making the sign for Pig - and all the children copied her.

Fantastic results

Recently, I had a call from the nursery. They wanted to move Daisy up to the toddler room, three months before she hit the right age.

Where is Olli?

Recently, I had a call from the nursery. They wanted to move Daisy up to the toddler room, three months before she hit the right age.

I know that's just one term early, but it's actually about 15 percent of her life to date. I went in to discuss it with the manager, her key worker and the nursery owner, and asked what made them think Daisy needed an early move? "Everything" said the manager. "The words she is coming out with are amazing."

Well, that puts the seal on it. Signing cannot have held back Daisy's language development. The spoken two-word combinations came in the first week of March, way ahead of schedule, and before that she was putting signs together like Where dog and Baby cry, so verbalising them was definitely on the cards.

Daisy helps out

During the Easter holidays, Daisy started signing to ask for her nappy to be changed. She obviously took this new sign to nursery because her key worker told me she had seen Daisy use it. One of her pals was having a tantrum because he had to go and have his nappy changed. Daisy went over to him and signed Change. Her key worker told me she was really quite impatient with him. The key worker interpreted it as Daisy telling the boy to go and get his nappy changed. Within a couple of days all the toddlers in her room had added Change to their signing vocabulary.

Real progress for everyone in the group.

How to use this book

This book is original in its approach to teaching sign language because, unlike other books, it does not just rely on photographs and descriptions of the signs.

The signs used in this book have been specially selected to be relevant to the needs of both carers and children and they are then woven into a series of stories. Olli, the monkey, communicates with those around him by using sign language rather than just speech. Olli is an easily recognisable character with whom children can readily identify.

How to learn each sign

The signs have been incorporated into four stories about Olli, the monkey and his family and friends. Each story is prefaced by a vocabulary section, showing the new signs that are highlighted within that particular story.

To produce the sign, begin by looking at the picture and replicate the positions and shapes of the hands, arms, body and facial expressions exactly as you see them. Then read the description to understand how the sign should be performed. Arrows on some pictures help you to see how the hands should move, and in which directions.

Building vocabulary

In the first story, Olli and the Bouncy Bed, all the words that are to be signed appear in red. For example, the word Monkey is highlighted in red. This means it corresponds to a sign in the vocabulary section for that story.

In the second and subsequent stories, signs already learnt in previous stories are written in blue while new signs are again highlighted in red.

By learning a few signs at a time and using them when reading the stories, to help you practice and remember them, you can quickly build up a vocabulary of over 100 signs.

Using the signs with your children

To begin with you may not need such a large vocabulary. Use the book to choose signs that are relevant to you and concentrate on those.

The best way to get your children to recognise the signs is to read the stories to them every day, and use the signs whenever they appear in red or blue. Once you have learnt all the signs in the book you can read the stories again and use all the signs, whether they appear in red or blue, or not.

Repetition is the key

Remember to support your signs with the spoken word whenever possible. Your children will learn much more quickly from the total-communication approach, using both your voice and the signs.

As mentioned in the Helpful Hints section, many people begin with just a few basic signs such as Milk and More and then gradually introduce other signs as the children begin to recognise and use them.

Additionally, try to use picture books and objects from your surroundings when introducing new signs. This will help to support the links between signs and objects. For example, when using the sign for Cat you might point to a picture of a cat before signing it, or maybe point to a real cat, if you have one.

Learning a new language is a great experience, so get everyone involved. It is an excellent bonding exercise to get everyone in the family learning and using the signs together. Don't worry if your child's first attempts at signs are not exact copies of your own, they will improve with gentle correction and repetition.

Olli says: In this book our signers are right-handed. If you are left-handed then you should reproduce the signs using your left hand as the dominant one.

Hand shapes

In order to help you create the signs shown on the vocabulary pages, here are some of the most commonly used hand shapes. To the right is an example of how signs are presented in the vocabulary sections throughout the book. The direction of movement is shown by the red arrows on the vocabulary pictures. Double arrowheads indicate where two repeat movements are required.

Bent hand

Bunched hand

'C' hand

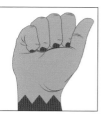

Clawed hand

Closed hand

DOG
Two 'N' hands pointing down make small downwards movement

Fist

Flat hand

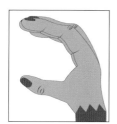

Full 'C' hand

'M' hand

'N' hand

'O' hand

Open hand

'V' hand

'Y' hand

When looking at vocabulary pages you will notice the book sometimes refers to things like 'N' Hands or Clawed Hand. When you see any references like this, look at these pictures, as creating the hand shape will help you to produce the sign accurately.

Meet the

The characters of Olli, the Little Monkey, and his family and friends, are used throughout the book to teach you the signs and help you remember them.

Finger spelling is the backbone of sign language. It can be used to spell the names of people, places and objects. In British Sign Language, both hands are used together, to create the 26 letters of the alphabet.

It doesn't matter whether you are right-handed or left-handed so long as you are consistent, and you don't keep changing hands half way through spelling a word. This can become very confusing to the person trying to read your finger spelling.

Because this book is aimed at those with, or working with, young children, the finger spelling in the stories has been kept to a minimum. However, even though the names of the characters have not been highlighted in the text as words to be signed, there is no reason why you cannot finger spell the names of the various characters. This will help to improve everyone's finger spelling abilities and increase children's literacy skills.

The first things we will learn are the vowels, A, E, I, O and U, together with a few other letters. To make life

easier, each member of Olli's immediate family has been given a name of four letters and each of their names begins with one of the five vowels. Anni is Olli's mother, Eddi is Olli's father, Iggi is Olli's older brother and Ulli is Olli's baby sister.

Assuming that you are right-handed, the vowels are represented by the fingers and thumb of the left hand and are indicated by pointing at them in turn using the index finger of your right hand. Reverse this process if you are left-handed.

Let's begin learning to finger spell with Anni, the name of Mummy Monkey.

A is the first of the vowels and is signed by pointing the index finger of the right hand at the thumb of the left hand as in the example above right.

Now let's add the other letters N, N, I. Now put them all together...

Congratulations. You have just finger spelt your first word: ANNI

Now try spelling the names of the other members of the monkey family using the finger spelling chart on page 14 to help:

A

N

N

I

Olli says: **Can you finger spell the names for all of my family?**

ANNI
EDDI
IGGI
OLLI
ULLI

In addition to the five vowels that you already know, you have added four other letters to your vocabulary.

Why not practice your new skill by spelling your own name and the names of your family and friends.

Don't worry if you are all fingers and thumbs at first. This is quite natural. Take it slowly. It is more important to be accurate than to be super fast.

Watch out for those vowels. It is very easy to get I, O and U mixed up.

monkeys

Iggi

Eddi

Anni

Grandad

Grandma

My name is Olli

Ulli

Daxi

13

Finger Spelling

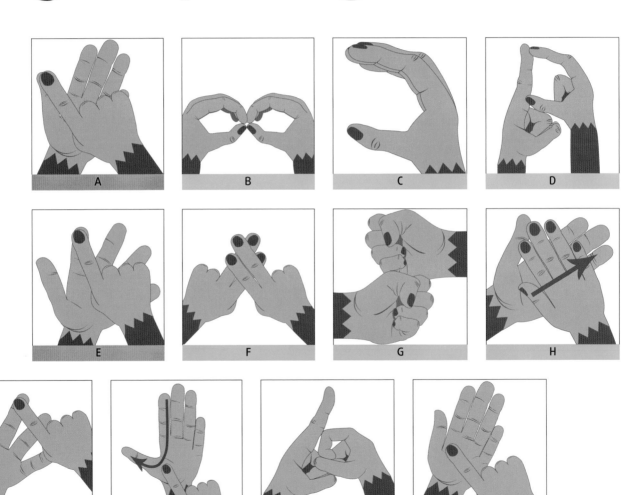

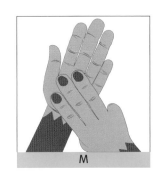

M

N

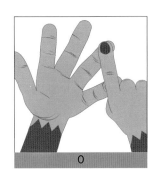

O

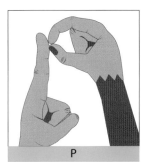

P

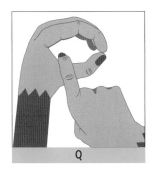

Q

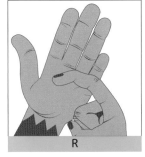

R

S

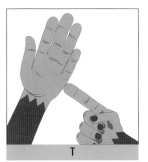

T

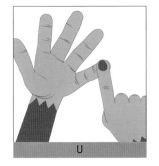

U

V

W

X

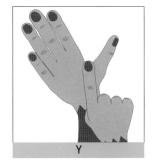

Y

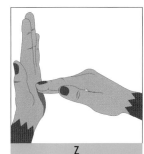

Z

15

Olli and the **bouncy bed** - vocabulary

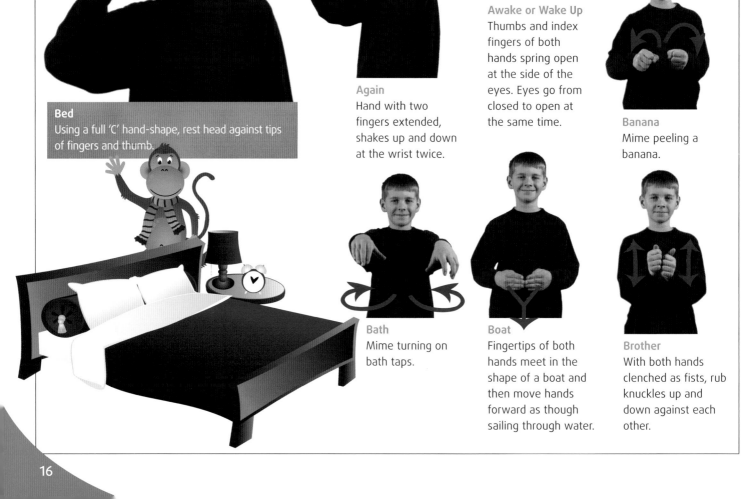

Bed
Using a full 'C' hand-shape, rest head against tips of fingers and thumb.

Again
Hand with two fingers extended, shakes up and down at the wrist twice.

Awake or Wake Up
Thumbs and index fingers of both hands spring open at the side of the eyes. Eyes go from closed to open at the same time.

Banana
Mime peeling a banana.

Bath
Mime turning on bath taps.

Boat
Fingertips of both hands meet in the shape of a boat and then move hands forward as though sailing through water.

Brother
With both hands clenched as fists, rub knuckles up and down against each other.

Butter
'N' shaped hand butters back and forth across the flat palm of the other hand, as if buttering bread.

Clever
Tip of thumb moves from left to right across forehead.

Cold
Shiver as if it's really cold.

Daddy
Tap 'F' twice.

Doctor
Check for pulse.

Family
Finger spell 'F' and move in a circle clockwise away from the body.

Food
The bunched fingers of one hand tap the lips twice, as if eating something.

Home or House
The tips of the fingers of both 'flat' hands touch together to form a roof.

Enough
With bent hand, tap the back of the fingers twice underneath the chin.

Ill
The fists of both hands, with little fingers extended, start at the top of the chest and move down to the stomach.

Hot
(Used for hot food, water, objects) Clawed hand moves across the mouth from left to right.

Milk
Both hands closed, with thumbs held up, move up and down as if milking a cow.

Hungry
A flat right hand rubs the stomach in a circular motion.

Little
Flat hand with palm downwards, indicates the height of a child.

Monkey
Hands scratch under arms.

More
Fingers of flat right hand tap the back of the flat left hand twice.

Mummy
The three fingers of an 'M' hand tap the top of head twice.

Sister
With one hand in a fist, index finger extended and slightly bent, tap the index finger on the nose twice.

Noisy
Fist with Index finger extended moves in a clockwise circle at the side of the head.

Quietly
With both hands in the 'O' shape begin with the tips of the index fingers and thumbs of both hands touching in front of you. Then slowly draw them down and apart.

Sign
With both hands open and palms facing each other, slightly apart, rotate forwards in small circles in front of the chest so that when one hand is up the other is down and vice-versa.

Time
Index finger points to watch.

Toast
With both hands flat, move upwards, as if popping out of a toaster.

Water
With an 'O' hand, brush the index finger and thumb down the cheek, twice.

Tree
The elbow of the right arm rests on the back of the left hand. The open right hand then twists slightly, as if in a breeze.

Olli and the **bouncy bed**

Olli the little monkey, lived in a house at the top of a tall, tall tree with Mummy Monkey, Daddy Monkey and the rest of his family.

Olli was a very clever little monkey. He didn't need to use his voice to talk to his family. Olli could talk to his friends and his family just by using his hands.

Olli used his hands to make signs. The little monkey would chat with his friends and family using signs.

The clever little monkey loved to chatter. Olli would sign about the animals and birds he had seen in the jungle below the tree house. The little monkey's hands could describe and make the shape of any animal or bird he had seen. Olli could sign to his friends about school, his family and even his favourite food. Whatever he wanted to say, the little monkey only needed to sign and everybody understood him.

Every morning, Mummy Monkey would wake up Olli and the family at the same time.

But Olli was always the first of the monkey family to wake up, jump out of bed and run to the bathroom to fill

the bath with hot water.
Having a bath was such fun. The bathroom always got so hot and full of steam. It was like a jungle.

While he was in the bath, Olli liked to pretend that he was the captain of a boat, sailing down a dangerous river, looking for hungry crocodiles.

The little monkey would sing and sign his favourite bath time song as loudly as he could.

> Every morning bath time
> The water makes you clean
> But watch out for the crocodiles
> Swimming up the stream
>
> Hungry Hungry Crocodiles
> Nibbling at your toes
> Snippy Snappy Crocodiles
> Biting off your nose
>
> Monkey sees the crocodiles
> Time to run away
> Clever little monkey
> Lives another day
>
> Hungry Hungry Crocodiles
> Nibbling at your toes
> Snippy Snappy Crocodiles
> Biting off your nose

Olli sang and signed the song again and again until the bathwater went very cold and all the Monkey Family were awake!

Sometimes Olli could be a very noisy monkey. After his bath, it was time for breakfast.

Downstairs in the kitchen, Olli could smell the toast that Daddy Monkey was making for the family.
If there was one thing that Olli liked more than a bath it was food.

All monkeys love toast, especially when it is hot and spread thickly with butter and sliced bananas. Olli quickly ate his toast and drank his glass of cold milk, but he was still hungry and wanted more.

Sometimes Olli could be a very hungry monkey. "Daddy, Could I have more toast, please?" said Olli. Daddy Monkey said: "No. You have had enough to eat. If you eat any more you will be ill and then we will have to phone a doctor. Now go to your bedroom and have a rest."

But Olli didn't want to lie quietly on his bed. He wanted to play his favourite game with his brother, Iggi

Olli says: Sometimes I can be a very noisy monkey. I hope the big green crocodile doesn't hear me.

and sister, Ulli. Olli loved his bed because it was so springy and great for bouncing on. Olli would bounce so high that he could touch the ceiling.

Sometimes Olli could be a very playful monkey. Quietly at first, the three little monkeys began to bounce on the bed.

The old bed began to creak and groan. While they bounced, Olli and his brother and sister sang and signed a song they knew about "Five Little Monkeys bouncing on the bed"

Five little monkeys bouncing on the bed
One fell off and bumped his head
Mummy phoned the Doctor and the Doctor said
"No more monkeys bouncing on the bed"

Four little monkeys bouncing on the bed
One fell off and bumped his head
Mummy phoned the Doctor and the Doctor said
"No more monkeys bouncing on the bed"

Three little monkeys bouncing on the bed
One fell off and bumped his head
Mummy phoned the Doctor and the Doctor said
"No more monkeys bouncing on the bed"

Two little monkeys bouncing on the bed
One fell off and bumped his head
Mummy phoned the Doctor and the Doctor said
"No more monkeys bouncing on the bed"

One little monkey bouncing on the bed
He fell off and bumped his head
Mummy phoned the Doctor and the Doctor said
"No more monkeys bouncing on the bed"

As the monkeys bounced higher and higher the singing got noisier and noisier until suddenly there was a loud "PING" as one of the bed springs shot through the mattress and catapulted Olli high into the air, across the room and onto the top of the wardrobe.

The singing stopped and everything went very, very quiet.

Mummy and Daddy ran up the stairs and into the bedroom. "What is going on?" cried Mummy. "Olli are you hurt?" "No Mummy" said Olli, "I just bumped my head, that's all"

"Well, it's lucky that you haven't broken anything, apart from the bed!" laughed Daddy, "But I think that is the last time we have any monkeys bouncing on the bed."

Olli says:
You have just learnt your first group of words. Well done.

23

Olli and the **bus** - vocabulary

Animals
With clawed hands, palms facing downwards, make forward movements as though creeping through the jungle.

Biscuit
Bunched hand taps the elbow twice.

Building Blocks
Two full 'C' hands build an imaginary tower upwards, moving one on top of the other twice.

Ball
Hands outline the shape of a ball.

Bus
Mime turning a large steering wheel.

Change
Two closed hands rotate forwards over each other to change places.

Clean
Left flat hand, palm face upwards, is brushed clean with blade of flat right hand.

Clothes
Open hands brush twice down the body.

Day
With both hands flat and palms facing towards you, begin with one hand in front of the other and arms level, then swing hands up and apart from elbows.

Dinner
'N' hands move back and forth to mouth.

Don't Like
Flat hand pats chest twice while head shakes.

Finished
Hands clenched in fists with thumbs extended, rotate in small, sideways circles in front of you.

Friends
Hands clasp together and move up and down as if shaking hands with yourself.

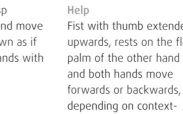

Help
Fist with thumb extended upwards, rests on the flat palm of the other hand and both hands move forwards or backwards, depending on context—I help you or you help me.

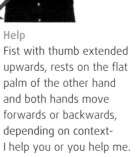

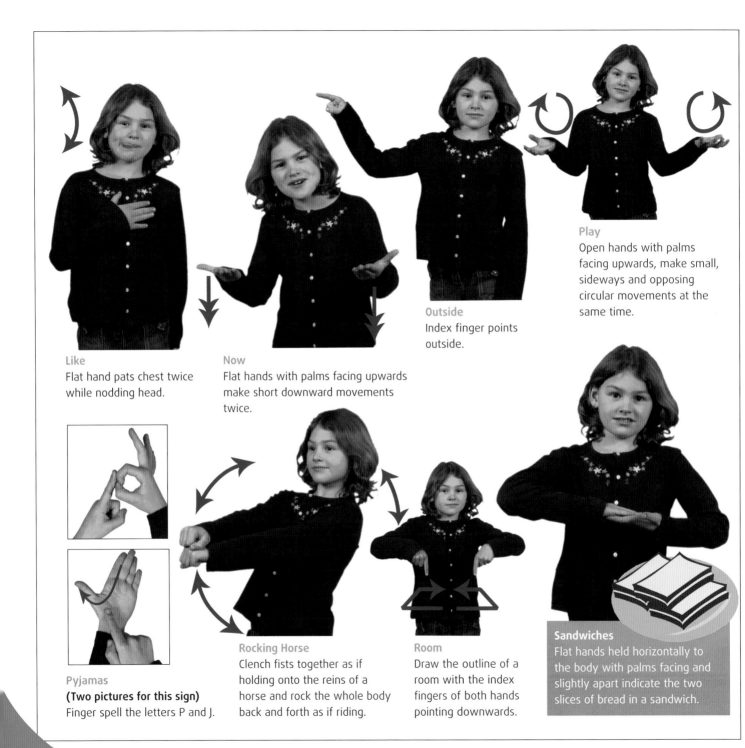

Like
Flat hand pats chest twice while nodding head.

Now
Flat hands with palms facing upwards make short downward movements twice.

Outside
Index finger points outside.

Play
Open hands with palms facing upwards, make small, sideways and opposing circular movements at the same time.

Pyjamas
(Two pictures for this sign)
Finger spell the letters P and J.

Rocking Horse
Clench fists together as if holding onto the reins of a horse and rock the whole body back and forth as if riding.

Room
Draw the outline of a room with the index fingers of both hands pointing downwards.

Sandwiches
Flat hands held horizontally to the body with palms facing and slightly apart indicate the two slices of bread in a sandwich.

Sorry
Closed hand rubs in small circle, clockwise on the chest.

Sun
Look at a raised bunched hand which then springs open, like rays of the sun.

Teddy Bear
Mime cuddling a teddy bear and twist the upper body slightly from side to side.

Thank You
Move flat hand with palm facing inwards, away and down from the mouth.

Train
Mime the action of a train using flat hands at either side of the body.

What
With index finger pointing upwards and palm facing outwards, waggle the hand from side to side.

Work or Job
With both hands flat and thumbs pointing upwards, cross the hands horizontally in front of you, to form an X and then tap the right hand down onto the top of the left hand twice.

Yellow
Finger spell Y.

Olli and the bus

It was a beautiful day in the jungle and the sun was shining. Olli, the little monkey, wanted to go outside and play with his brother and sister but Mummy said Olli could play outside later - but first he had to help tidy the house.

There was always lots of work to be done in the tree house.

Olli's job was to tidy his bedroom at the very top of the tree house. His brother and sister kept their rooms tidy but Olli's room was such a mess. Mummy didn't like mess: "Olli, I want that room clean by dinner time. Go to your bedroom right now."

Olli looked at his untidy bedroom and just didn't know where to start.

The floor was covered with clothes and the bed was piled high with toys. The building blocks needed stacking, next to the rocking horse, and the train had to be put back in its box under the bed.

There was so much work to do. The little monkey gave a big sigh and began to work. First, he put the ball back in the toy box, and then he picked up his Teddy Bear and placed him on the end of the bed where he belonged.

It was then that Olli saw something shiny and yellow sticking out from under the corner of the bed.
"I wonder what that is?" said Olli As he got closer he saw that the yellow thing was one of his favourite toys: a yellow bus.

Olli was so excited to find the bus again that he forgot all about cleaning his room and began to play.

The little monkey liked to play.

Olli pretended he was driving the bus through the countryside, meeting lots of different animals and making new friends. As he played he began to sing.

Monkey and I went driving
The yellow bus one day
Chatting to the animals we met
All along the way

"Good morning" said the brown cow
"Will you stop and play?"
"I'm sorry" said the monkey
"I don't have time today"

Monkey and I went driving
The yellow bus one day
Chatting to the animals we met
All along the way

Next we met a blackbird
Singing in a tree
"I'm sorry" said the monkey
"I don't have time for tea"

Monkey and I went driving
The yellow bus one day
Chatting to the animals we met
All along the way

Then we saw a rabbit
Going to the shop
"I'm sorry" said the monkey
"I don't have time to stop"

Monkey and I went driving
The yellow bus one day
Chatting to the animals we met
All along the way

Olli was so busy singing and playing with the yellow bus, that he didn't notice when it was dinner-time. The little monkey realised that he had been playing for a long time and his room still wasn't clean.

Quietly, Olli tiptoed downstairs to the kitchen. Mummy was busy making dinner. "Hello Olli" she said. "Have you finished tidying your room?" "Sorry Mummy, but I found my yellow bus and I had so much fun playing that I forgot the time. I promise I will finish the job after dinner."

"That's a good boy" said Mummy "But this time I will help, to make sure that the work gets done and you don't start playing with the yellow bus again."

Olli says: It's been a tiring day and I'm really looking forward to eating my banana sandwiches.

"Thank you Mummy" said Olli as he tucked in to his dinner of banana sandwiches.

Finally, when Mummy and Olli had finished tidying the bedroom, Olli was very tired from all the hard work. The little monkey yawned as Mummy said "Time for bed. Go to your bedroom and change into your pyjamas and I will bring you some supper."

Minutes later, Olli was tucked up in bed drinking a glass of cold milk and munching on a biscuit.

Mummy softly sang and signed the Monkey's Lullaby as the little monkey drifted gently off to sleep, worn out after his busy day.

Time for bed
The Monkey said
Time for you to sleep
Time to count the stars above
Time to count the sheep

The moon is bright
Dream all night
See you in the morning light

Time for bed
The Monkey said
Time for bed I say
Time for you to close your eyes
It's been a busy day

The moon is bright
Dream all night
See you in the morning light

Time for bed
The Monkey said
Time for you to sleep
Time to count the stars above
Time to count the sheep

Olli says:
Driving the bus through the countryside, I met lots of different animals and made lots of new friends. Can you remember who they were?

Olli and the farm - vocabulary

Baby
Mime holding a baby and rock arms from side to side.

Black
Closed hand moves down the side of the cheek.

Car
Hands mime turning a steering wheel as if driving.

Cat
Flex the fingers of clawed hands which move out from either side of the mouth to show whiskers.

Coat
Mime putting a coat on over the shoulders.

Colour
One 'C' hand makes circular movements, anti-clockwise in front of the body.

Cow
Place 'Y'-shaped hands either side of the head with the thumbs touching the temples.

Different
With both hands as fists and index fingers extended, place both index fingers together, side by side, pointing outwards. Move the hands up and away from each other.

Donkey
Place flat hands on top of the head with palms facing forward as though they are the ears of a donkey.

Dog
With two 'N' hands pointing downwards, make small downward movements, twice.

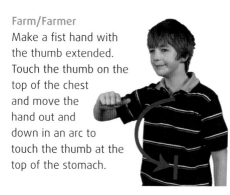

Farm/Farmer
Make a fist hand with the thumb extended. Touch the thumb on the top of the chest and move the hand out and down in an arc to touch the thumb at the top of the stomach.

Duck
The fingers of a bunched hand open and close onto the thumb in front of the chin, miming the beak of a duck opening and closing.

Hat
Mime putting on a hat.

Funny
Cross two 'C' hands at the wrist in front of the face, with the opening of the 'C' held horizontally towards the mouth. Imagine each hand is your lower jaw and move from side to side as though laughing.

Goodbye
Wave Goodbye.

Happy
Both flat hands are held horizontally to the body with palms facing and hands slightly apart, the right hand then claps against the left as it brushes up the hand towards the left wrist, twice.

Pig
A closed hand makes small circles in front of the nose.

Look
The fingers of a 'V' hand move forward from the eye.

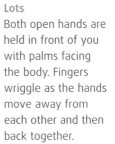

Lots
Both open hands are held in front of you with palms facing the body. Fingers wriggle as the hands move away from each other and then back together.

Make
The right hand fist strikes the left hand fist twice, in a circular motion.

Nappy
The fingers of both N hands tap twice at either side of the waist.

Park
The edge of a flat hand with the thumb facing in, taps twice against the shoulder.

Please
A flat hand moves away and down from the mouth.

Quickly
Right index finger bounces off the left index finger.

Roundabout
One fist with index finger extended and pointing upwards and one fist with index finger extended and pointing downwards, move round each other in a clockwise direction.

Same
Fists of both hands with index fingers extended and pointing forwards are brought together so that index fingers are touching side by side.

See-Saw
A straight arm with a flat hand moves up and down, imitating the movement of a see-saw.

Sheep
Fists with little fingers extended make the shape of horns at the side of the head.

Swings
With fists closed, arms swing back and forth at side of body, imitating being on a swing.

Stop
Flat hands are held out in front of you with palms facing forwards. Fingers and thumbs then snap shut to form bunched hands.

Slide
Flat hand mimes going down a slide.

White
The index finger and thumb of an 'O' hand make two short forward movements on the collar bone near the neck.

35

Olli and the farm

It was early in the morning, but everyone in the Monkey Family was out of bed.

Yesterday, Mummy had promised to take Olli and his baby sister, Ulli, to the park on the other side of town.

Olli had never been to the park before but he had been told by Iggi, his older brother, that there were swings, roundabouts, a see-saw and a big, big slide as tall as a house.

Olli had already had his bath and was just finishing his toast when Mummy asked him to fetch a clean nappy from upstairs so she could change his sister, before they left for the park.

Olli quickly found the nappy then got his coat and ran to the car.

Mummy drove the car quickly through the town and out into the countryside. On the way Olli saw a field full of strange, white, fluffy, animals.

Olli thought the animals were very funny and asked his Mummy: "What are those funny white things?"

"They are sheep" said Mummy, "Their fluffy coats make wool so that we can have hats and jumpers to stop us feeling cold in winter."

Mummy told Olli that the sheep belonged to a man called a farmer. "The farmer cares for all the animals, and makes sure they have food and water."

All the sheep were the same white colour. Then Olli spotted one little sheep standing with his Mummy in the far corner of the field. This sheep was different from the others. His wool wasn't white; his wool was a beautiful black colour.
Mummy taught Olli and his sister a song about a sheep, called "Baa Baa Black Sheep", which they sang and signed together.

> Baa Baa Black Sheep
> Have You Any Wool?
> Yes Sir, Yes Sir
> Three Bags Full
> One for the Master
> One for the Dame
> And One for the Little Boy
> Who Lives Down the Lane

Olli said, "Please Mummy, stop the car at the farm so that we can look at all the animals." So Mummy stopped the car at the side of the road and together they began to count the different animals that they could see in the fields.
Together they counted the farm animals.

They counted:
6 Donkeys
5 Cows
4 Ducks
3 Pigs
2 Cats and
1 Dog

Plus lots and lots of sheep.

When they had finished counting Mummy said: "I think it's time we got back in the car. We don't want to be late getting to the park. Olli climbed into the car and waved to the sheep. "Goodbye sheep" he called, "See you next time."
By the time they got home from the park, Olli was a very happy monkey.

Olli says: Mummy told me that the sheep belonged to a man called a Farmer. "The Farmer cares for all the animals, and makes sure they have food and water".

Happy Birthday Olli - vocabulary

Aeroplane
A 'Y' hand moves through the air as though an aeroplane taking off.

Afternoon
The index finger and middle finger of an 'N' hand touch the chin and then flick outwards.

Birthday
Flat hands on either side of the waist, with fingertips pointing downwards, move up the body and then outwards.

Blue
The index finger of one hand makes small movements back and forth on the back of the other hand to indicate blue veins.

Book
Flat hands with palms together, open to palms facing upwards as though opening a book.

Boy
The index finger of the right hand points left and then moves from right to left just beneath the lower lip.

Brown
Bent hand opens and closes onto the thumb at the side of the face.

Cake
Tips of a clawed hand tap the back of the other hand.

Excited
Tips of clawed hands move quickly up and down chest in opposing directions.

Girl
With index finger pointing upwards and palm facing forwards, brush the finger down the side of the cheek twice.

Good
A fist with thumb extended upwards, makes a small forward movement.

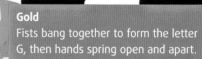

Gold
Fists bang together to form the letter G, then hands spring open and apart.

Grandad (Two signs)
Fingerspell the letters G and F.

Grandma (Two signs)
Fingerspell the letters G and M.

Green
Finger tips of right flat hand with palm facing down, move up the left arm from the wrist towards the elbow.

Hello
Wave hello.

I Love You (Three signs)
Point to yourself to sign I. Then cross your hands over your chest to sign Love. Then point to the person you are talking about to sign You.

Ice Cream
A closed hand makes short downward movements near an open mouth with tongue out, as if licking an ice cream.

Morning
Tips of bent hand move from the left to the right side of chest.

Name
The fingers of an 'N' hand touch the forehead and then twist outwards so that the palm is facing forwards.

New
With left flat hand horizontal and palm facing inwards, brush the back of the right flat hand up and against the palm of the left.

Orange
A clawed hand near the side of the face opens and closes as if squeezing a juicy orange.

Party
Two 'Y' hands move in small opposing circles near the side of the head.

Pink
Make fist with the palm facing forwards, and index finger extended. Touch the side of the cheek with the tip of the index finger and then rotate the hand so that the palm faces backwards.

Purple
Fingerspell the letter P, then tap the left index finger with the right 'O' hand, twice.

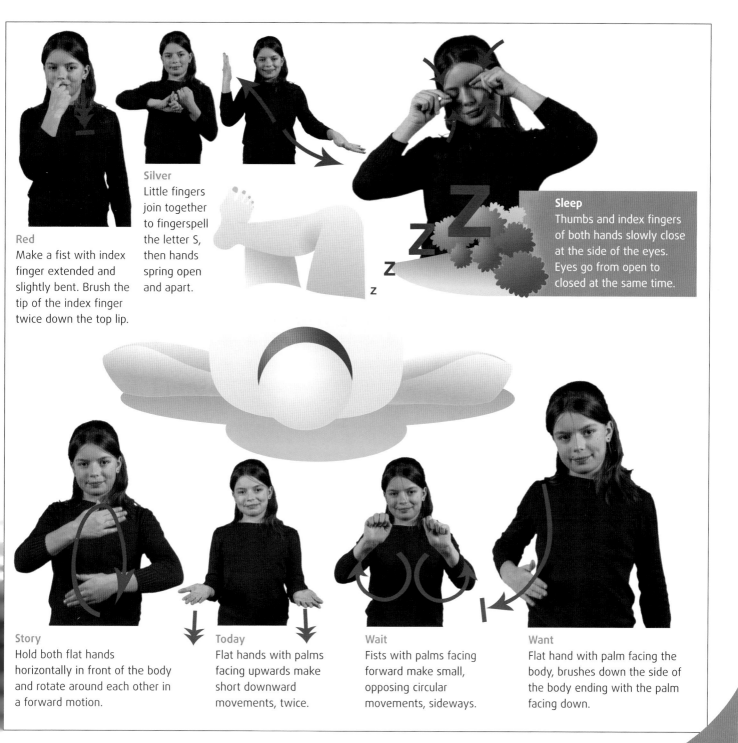

Red
Make a fist with index finger extended and slightly bent. Brush the tip of the index finger twice down the top lip.

Silver
Little fingers join together to fingerspell the letter S, then hands spring open and apart.

Sleep
Thumbs and index fingers of both hands slowly close at the side of the eyes. Eyes go from open to closed at the same time.

Story
Hold both flat hands horizontally in front of the body and rotate around each other in a forward motion.

Today
Flat hands with palms facing upwards make short downward movements, twice.

Wait
Fists with palms facing forward make small, opposing circular movements, sideways.

Want
Flat hand with palm facing the body, brushes down the side of the body ending with the palm facing down.

Happy Birthday Olli

Olli was very, very excited. It was early in the morning but the little monkey had been awake for hours. He couldn't sleep. Today was a very special day – today was Olli's birthday.

Olli couldn't wait to open his presents.

Mummy and Daddy had asked him what he would like for his birthday. Olli had told his Mummy that he wanted a dog.

"I want a dog to play with, and to be my best friend." Mummy laughed and told Olli that he would have to wait and see.

All that morning Mummy was busy in the kitchen making the food for Olli's party that afternoon. There would be jelly, ice cream, banana sandwiches and of course a big, big birthday cake with candles, and plenty of orange squash to drink.

In the lounge Olli was busy, helping Daddy decorate the room with balloons and streamers of different colours. They were red, yellow, blue, green, pink and purple. When they had finished, Daddy said: "Thank you for helping, Olli. You are a good boy."

At 3 o'clock that afternoon the doorbell rang. Olli ran to open the door. Standing in the doorway were Olli's Grandma and Grandad, each carrying a silver box tied up with a gold bow. "Happy Birthday Olli," they cried. "Hello Grandma, hello Grandad," said Olli, "Please come in."

The Monkey Family gathered round the table as Olli began to open his birthday presents. Iggi, his brother, had bought him a new train for his train set and Ulli, his baby sister gave him a red London bus.

44

Olli was so happy and excited that he couldn't wait to see what Grandma and Grandad had brought him. He quickly tore off the paper and opened the lid of the first box. Inside was a silver toy aeroplane with Olli's name written in large blue letters along each wing. "Oh, thank you Grandad," said Olli, "My very own aeroplane."

"Now it's time for my present," said Grandma. Olli wondered what Grandma could have brought him. "Go on, open it," said Grandma. As he peeled open the parcel Olli saw that it was a book. "It's a story book," said Grandma. "Would you like me to read you a story?" she asked. "Yes please," said Olli.

The Monkey Family listened quietly as Grandma read them all a story from the book.
When the story was finished, Daddy told Olli to close his eyes and wait. The little monkey did as he was told and waited with his eyes tightly shut.

"Now," said Daddy, "Open your eyes." Olli opened his eyes. In front of him, wagging its tail, was a tiny little dog with big, big, brown eyes and a long pink tongue. At last Olli had a new friend.

"This is your new dog, her name is Daxi," said Mummy. Daxi jumped up and licked Olli's nose. "Good girl," said Olli, "Welcome to your new home."

"Oh, Thank you Mummy, Thank you Daddy. This is the best birthday ever. I love you."

Everyone sat down at the table to eat the special birthday tea. When it was time to blow out the candles on the cake they began to sing and sign the special birthday song to Olli.

Olli was a very happy monkey.

Olli says:
I've had a brilliant birthday and I really liked my presents, especially my new dog Daxi

Birthday boy
Birthday Boy
Happy day to you
With biscuits cake and orange squash
With love from me to you

Birthday boy
Birthday boy
With cake and cards we say
Make a wish with eyes shut tight
On this your special day

Birthday boy
Birthday Boy
Happy day to you
With biscuits cake and orange squash
With love from me to you

Birthday boy
Birthday boy
A year older now
You're growing up
Birthday boy
It's time to take a bow
Birthday boy
Birthday Boy
Happy day to you
With biscuits cake and orange squash
With love from me to you

Afterword  by **Janey Lee Grace**

I'm so inspired by this book, knowing how important communication really is. So many parents and care-givers think the answer is to plonk a toddler in front of the TV - the electric nanny - but, to be able to actively participate in their joy of learning, in the early years, is so much more rewarding. Stories, singing, actions and rhymes all play an important part in developing language skills, and sign language adds another wonderful dimension.

I've seen many a furious toddler having an absolute tantrum - not because they're naughty but because their verbal skills simply aren't developed enough for them to communicate to their bewildered parents exactly what it is they need. Before escalating into full-blown rage, it may have started off as the child simply needing a drink or a cuddle.

Garry's fantastic, easy-to-use programme bridges that gap, and also teaches a valuable skill.

Janey Lee Grace

BBC Radio 2 presenter and co-host of Steve Wright in the Afternoon.
Author of: Imperfectly Natural Woman - getting life right the natural way. Crown House Publishing.

About the author

Garry Slack is a fully qualified Communication Support Worker for deaf people, and has extensive experience of supporting both deaf and deaf-blind people in many different situations.

He has developed and delivered Deaf Awareness and Sign Language workshops to people of all ages, including popular classes for mothers and babies. In 2005 he was commissioned by Lincolnshire County Council, Early Years and Childcare Services, to deliver training in non-verbal communication to the child-minders and care workers of Lincolnshire.

Garry lives in Stamford in Lincolnshire with his partner and four sausage dogs.

A big thankyou...

I would like to take this opportunity to thank all of the people who have helped to make this project a reality.

Thank you to Siân Lloyd and Janey Lee Grace for their invaluable contributions. Athol Dipple of 'Wild and Woolly' and David Tovey, 'The Puppetman', for their advice and support. Matt Maddock for his photographic skills, the models Ralph, Lydia, Jordan, Eloise and their families. Chris Young for designing the "Sausage Dog Publishing" logo and thanks also to the Art and Design Department of New College Stamford. Thanks to Sue Otter and all at the Lincolnshire County Council - Children's Services for their support and encouragement. John Owens of Business Link Lincolnshire and Rutland for his advice and all the stars at dsquared, Karis and Richard in particular, for their fantastic work and sense of humour! Neville and Glenys Walkley, Trustees of Deaf Lincs for their friendship and continued support, and finally a very special thank you to Johnny for all his hard work and patience!

Index of signs

Animals
Animal p24
Cat p32
Cow p32
Dog p33
Donkey p33
Duck p33
Monkey p18
Pig p34
Sheep p35

Clothes
Change p24
Clothes p25
Coat p32
Hat p33
Nappy p34
Pyjamas p26

Colours
Black p32
Blue p38
Brown p38
Colour p32
Gold p39
Green p39
Orange p40
Pink p40
Purple p40
Red p41
Silver p41
White p35
Yellow p27

Emotions and Feelings
Clever p17
Don't Like p25
Excited p39
Funny p33
Good p39
Happy p33
Ill p18
I Love You p39
Like p26
Sorry p27
Want p41

Everyday words
Help p25
Little p18
Look p34
Lots p34
Name p40
New p40
Please p34
Sign p19
Thank You p27
What? p27

Family
Baby p32
Boy p38
Brother p16
Daddy p17
Family p17
Friend p25
Girl p39
Granddad p39
Grandma p39
Mummy p18
Sister p19

Food
Bananas p16
Biscuit p24
Butter p17
Cake p38
Dinner p25
Drink p25
Enough p17
Food p17
Hungry p18
Ice Cream p40
Milk p18
More p18
Sandwich p26
Toast p19
Water p19

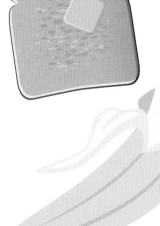